This journal belongs to

....

Ellie Claire® Gift & Paper Expressions
Franklin, TN 37067
EllieClaire.com
Ellie Claire is a registered trademark of Worthy Media, Inc.
Angels Watching Over Us Journal
© 2016 by Ellie Claire
Published by Ellie Claire, an imprint of Worthy Publishing Group,
a division of Worthy Media, Inc.

ISBN 978-1-63326-144-0

Compiled by Barbara Farmer
Designed by Lisa and Jeff Franke

Printed in China
1 2 3 4 5 6 7 8 9 – 20 19 18 17 16

You are helping us by praying for us. Then many people will give thanks because God has graciously answered so many prayers for our safety.

2 CORINTHIANS 1:11 NLT

The light of God surrounds me; the love of God enfolds me;
The power of God protects me; the presence of God watches over me.
Wherever I am, God is.

God is just: He will pay back trouble to those who trouble you and give relief to you who are troubled, and to us as well. This will happen when the Lord Jesus is revealed from heaven in blazing fire with his powerful angels.

2 THESSALONIANS 1:6-7 NIV

All God's angels come to us disguised.

James Russell Lowell

Why, anyone by just giving you a cup of water in my name is on our side.

MARK 9:41 THE MESSAGE

At the end of the day, let your mind settle on Him.... Thank Him for the good parts.... Question Him about the hard parts. Seek His mercy. Seek His strength. And as you close your eyes, take assurance in the promise: "He who watches over Israel will neither slumber nor sleep" (Psalm 121:4 NIV).

Max Lucado

....

....

....

....

....

....

....

....

....

....

....

....

....

....

....

....

....

*I can lie down and go to sleep, and I will wake up again,
because the Lord gives me strength.*

PSALM 3:5 NCV

Incredible as it may seem, God wants our companionship. He wants to have us close to Him. He wants to be a father to us, to shield us, to protect us, to counsel us, and to guide us in our way through life.

Billy Graham

··

··

··

··

··

··

··

··

··

··

··

··

··

··

*Let me hear of your unfailing love each morning, for I am trusting you.
Show me where to walk, for I give myself to you. Rescue me from my enemies, Lord;
I run to you to hide me. Teach me to do your will, for you are my God.
May your gracious Spirit lead me forward on a firm footing.*

PSALM 143:8-10 NLT

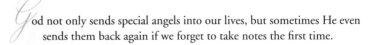

God not only sends special angels into our lives, but sometimes He even sends them back again if we forget to take notes the first time.

....

....

....

....

....

....

....

....

....

....

....

....

....

....

....

....

....

Dear friend, listen well to my words; tune your ears to my voice. Keep my message in plain view at all times. Concentrate! Learn it by heart! Those who discover these words live, really live; body and soul, they're bursting with health.

PROVERBS 4:20-22 THE MESSAGE

Insight is better than eyesight when it comes to seeing an angel.

For by him all things were created: things in heaven and on earth,
visible and invisible, whether thrones or powers or rulers or authorities;
all things were created by him and for him.

COLOSSIANS 1:16 NIV

The words "God is for us" proclaim God's undertaking to uphold and protect us when people and circumstances are threatening.... The simple statement "God is for us" is in truth one of the richest utterances that the Bible contains.

J. I. Packer

If God is for us, who can be against us? He who did not spare
His own Son, but delivered Him up for us all,
how shall He not with Him also freely give us all things?

ROMANS 8:31-32 NKJV

An angel can illuminate the thought and mind of man
by strengthening the power of vision.

Thomas Aquinas

The instructions of the LORD are perfect, reviving the soul. The decrees of the LORD are trustworthy, making wise the simple. The commandments of the LORD are right, bringing joy to the heart. The commands of the LORD are clear, giving insight for living.

PSALM 19:7-8 NLT

*When the soul has laid down its faults at the feet of God,
it feels as though it had wings.*

Eugénie de Guérin

....

....

....

....

....

....

....

....

....

....

....

....

....

....

....

Are you tired? Worn out? Burned out on religion? Come to me. Get away with me and you'll recover your life. I'll show you how to take a real rest.... I won't lay anything heavy or ill-fitting on you. Keep company with me and you'll learn to live freely and lightly.

MATTHEW 11:28-30 THE MESSAGE

The birds upon the tree-tops sing their song, the angels chant the chorus all day long,
The flowers in the garden blend their hue, so why shouldn't I,
why shouldn't you praise Him too?

....

....

....

....

....

....

....

....

....

....

....

....

....

....

....

....

....

*P*raise the LORD, you angels; praise the LORD's glory and power.
Praise the LORD for the glory of his name; worship the LORD because he is holy.

When you are in the dark, listen, and God will give you a very precious message for someone else when you get into the light.

Oswald Chambers

....

....

....

....

....

....

....

....

....

....

....

....

....

....

....

....

He comforts us in all our troubles so that we can comfort others. When they are troubled, we will be able to give them the same comfort God has given us.

2 CORINTHIANS 1:4 NLT

If trouble hearing the angels' song with thine ears,
try listening with thy heart.

Meriel Stelliger

....

....

....

....

....

....

....

....

....

....

....

....

....

....

....

....

....

My child, listen and be wise: Keep your heart on the right course.

PROVERBS 23:19 NLT

God's Word acts as a light for our paths. It can help scare off unwanted thoughts in our minds and protect us from the enemy.

Gary Smalley and John Trent

....

....

....

....

....

....

....

....

....

....

....

....

....

....

....

....

....

Your word is like a lamp for my feet and a light for my path.

PSALM 119:105 NCV

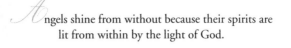

*Angels shine from without because their spirits are
lit from within by the light of God.*

Let your light shine before men, that they may see your good
deeds and praise your Father in heaven.

MATTHEW 5:16 NIV

The angels are the dispensers and administrators of the divine beneficence toward us.

John Calvin

....

....

....

....

....

....

....

....

....

....

....

....

....

....

....

....

....

....

....

....

....

....

....

....

....

....

....

....

....

....

....

....

....

....

*L*ove GOD, all you saints; GOD takes care
of all who stay close to him.

PSALM 31:23 THE MESSAGE

Friends are angels who lift our feet when our own wings have trouble remembering how to fly.

A friend is always loyal, and a brother is born to help in time of need.

PROVERBS 17:17 NLT

$\mathcal{W}$hat is the Lord saying? There's only one message: "Trust Me. Even when you don't understand and can't comprehend: trust Me!"

James Dolson

....

....

....

....

....

....

....

....

....

....

....

....

....

....

....

rust in the Lord with all your heart, and lean not on your own understanding; in all your ways acknowledge Him, and He shall direct your paths.

PROVERBS 3:5-6 NKJV

I pray for a child-like heart, for gentle, holy love,
For strength to do Thy will below, as angels do above.

All the angels are spirits who serve God and are sent
to help those who will receive salvation.

HEBREWS 1:14 NCV

God created us with an overwhelming desire to soar.... He designed us to be tremendously productive and "to mount up with wings like eagles," realistically dreaming of what He can do with our potential.

Carol Kent

....

....

....

....

....

....

....

....

....

....

....

....

....

....

....

....

....

Those who hope in the LORD will renew their strength. They will soar on wings like eagles; they will run and not grow weary, they will walk and not be faint.

ISAIAH 40:31 NIV

The reflective life is a way of living that heightens
our spiritual senses to all that is sacred.

Ken Gire

....

....

....

....

....

....

....

....

....

....

....

....

....

....

....

....

$\mathcal{I}$ will study your commandments and reflect on your ways.
I will delight in your decrees and not forget your word.

PSALM 119:15-16 NLT

I am Your servant! Everything I have is Yours. But even as I say that, I know You are serving me more than I am serving You. At Your command all the resources of heaven and earth are at my disposal, and even the angels help me.

Thomas à Kempis

So bless GOD, you angels, ready and able to fly at his bidding,
quick to hear and do what he says.

PSALM 103:20 THE MESSAGE

I often think flowers are the angels' alphabet whereby they write on hills and fields mysterious and beautiful lessons for us to feel and learn.

Louisa May Alcott

....

....

....

....

....

....

....

....

....

....

....

....

....

....

....

....

....

The heavens declare the glory of God, and the skies announce what his hands have made.... They have no speech or words; they have no voice to be heard. But their message goes out through all the world; their words go everywhere on earth.

PSALM 19:1, 3-4 NCV

If you have a tender message, or a loving word to say,
Do not wait till you forget it, but whisper it today.

Frank Herbert Sweet

Kind words are like honey—sweet to the soul
and healthy for the body.

PROVERBS 16:24 NLT

In some loving act of kindness as they show how much they care—
In the lives of folk around me I find God reflected there.

Cyrus E. Albertson

....
....
....
....
....
....
....
....
....
....
....
....
....
....
....
....
....

*W*hatever you do, work at it with all your heart,
as working for the Lord, not for men.

COLOSSIANS 3:23 NIV

Just as angels are attracted to the light of joy and kindness,
so too are miracles attracted to the lamp of faith and love.

Mary Augustine

*T*here is joy in the presence of the angels of God when
one sinner changes his heart and life.

Luke 15:10 ncv

If you believe in God, it is not too difficult to believe that He is concerned about the universe and all the events on this earth. But the really staggering message of the Bible is that this same God cares deeply about you and your identity and the events of your life.

Bruce Larson

An angel of the Lord appeared to them, and the glory of the Lord shone around them.... The angel said to them, "Do not be afraid. I bring you good news of great joy."

LUKE 2:9-10 NIV

Sleep, my child, and peace attend thee...all through the night.
Guardian angels God will send thee...all through the night.

Sir Harold Edwin Boulton

Bless GOD, all you armies of angels, alert to respond to whatever he wills. Bless GOD, all creatures, wherever you are—everything and everyone made by GOD.

PSALM 103:21-22 THE MESSAGE

God's holy beauty comes near you, like a spiritual scent, and it stirs your drowsing soul....
He creates in you the desire to find Him and run after Him—to follow wherever
He leads you, and to press peacefully against His heart wherever He is.

John of the Cross

God, you are my God. I search for you. I thirst for you like someone in a dry, empty land where there is no water. I have seen you in the Temple and have seen your strength and glory. Because your love is better than life, I will praise you.

PSALM 63:1-3 NCV

Sometimes, when the people around us make us feel like nothing, the best therapy we can find is in reflecting about how God sees us and what He has declared us to be before the angels in glory.

Tony Campolo

....

....

....

....

....

....

....

....

....

....

....

....

....

....

....

....

*B*eware that you don't look down on any of these little ones. For I tell you
that in heaven their angels are always in the presence of my heavenly Father.

MATTHEW 18:10 NLT

Hush! my dear, lie still and slumber. Holy angels guard thy bed!
Heavenly blessings without number gently falling on thy head.

Isaac Watts

*H*e has put his angels in charge of you to
watch over you wherever you go.

PSALM 91:11 NCV

God loves and cares for us, even to the least
event and smallest need of life.

Henry Edward Manning

Your heavenly Father already knows all your needs. Seek the Kingdom of God above all else, and live righteously, and he will give you everything you need.

MATTHEW 6:32-33 NLT

God's angels are as the winds, going and coming and ceasing to be [present] when their service is accomplished.

Amy Carmichael

....

....

....

....

....

....

....

....

....

....

....

....

....

....

....

....

....

....

....

Regarding the angels, he says, "He sends his angels like the winds, his servants like flames of fire."

HEBREWS 1:7 NLT

We are so preciously loved by God that we cannot even comprehend it. No created being can ever know how much and how sweetly and tenderly God loves them.

Julian of Norwich

*H*ow great is the love the Father has lavished on us, that we should be called children of God! And that is what we are!

1 JOHN 3:1 NIV

Angels can fly because they take themselves lightly.

G. K. Chesterton

*L*ook at the birds, free and unfettered, not tied down to a job description, careless in the care of God. And you count far more to him than birds.

Angels descending, bring from above
Echoes of mercy, whispers of love.

Fanny J. Crosby

God has chosen you and made you his holy people. He loves you. So you should always
clothe yourselves with mercy, kindness, humility, gentleness, and patience.

COLOSSIANS 3:12 NCV

When you come to the edge of all the light you have, and must take a step into the darkness of the unknown, believe that one of two things will happen. Either there will be something solid for you to stand on—or you will be taught how to fly.

Patrick Overton

....
....
....
....
....
....
....
....
....
....
....
....
....
....
....
....

*Now faith is being sure of what we hope for
and certain of what we do not see.*

HEBREWS 11:1 NIV

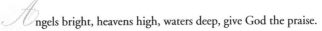

Angels bright, heavens high, waters deep, give God the praise.

Christopher Collins

Deep calls to deep in the roar of your waterfalls; all your waves and breakers have swept over me. By day the LORD directs his love, at night his song is with me—a prayer to the God of my life.

PSALM 42:7-8 NIV

You are a little less than angels, crown of creation, image of God. Each person is a revelation, a transfiguration, a waiting for Him to manifest Himself.

Edward Farrell

He who overcomes will, like them, be dressed in white. I will never blot out his name from the book of life, but will acknowledge his name before my Father and his angels.

REVELATION 3:5 NIV

From the tiny birds of the air and from the fragile lilies of the field we learn the same truth...: God takes care of His own. He knows our needs. He anticipates our crises. He is moved by our weaknesses. He stands ready to come to our rescue. And at just the right moment He steps in and proves Himself as our faithful heavenly Father.

Charles R. Swindoll

And the very hairs on your head are all numbered. So don't be afraid; you are more valuable to God than a whole flock of sparrows. I tell you the truth, everyone who acknowledges me publicly here on earth, the Son of Man will also acknowledge in the presence of God's angels.

LUKE 12:7-8 NLT

Angels have been said to be our neighbors. Often they may be our companions without our being aware of their presence.

Billy Graham

I tell you the truth, anything you did for even the least
of my people here, you also did for me.

MATTHEW 25:40 NCV

Amid ancient lore the Word of God stands unique and pre-eminent.
Wonderful in its construction, admirable in its adaptation, it contains truths that
a child may comprehend, and mysteries into which angels desire to look.

Frances Ellen Watkins Harper

*F*or who in all of heaven can compare with the LORD? What mightiest
angel is anything like the LORD? The highest angelic powers stand in awe of God.
He is far more awesome than all who surround his throne.

PSALM 89:6-7 NLT

God...will take care of you day and night forever.

Norman Vincent Peale

He will not let you stumble; the one who watches over you
will not slumber.... The LORD himself watches over you!
The LORD stands beside you as your protective shade.

PSALM 121:3, 5 NLT

Friendship is something that raised us almost above humanity. This love, free from instinct, free from all duties but those which love has freely assumed, almost wholly free from jealousy, and free without qualification from the need to be needed, is eminently spiritual. It is the sort of love one can imagine between angels.

C. S. Lewis

Two are better than one, because they have a good return for their work:
If one falls down, his friend can help him up.

ECCLESIASTES 4:9-10 NIV

Silently one by one, in the infinite meadow of heaven blossomed the lovely stars, the forget-me-nots of the angels.

Henry Wadsworth Longfellow

LORD, our Lord, how majestic is your name in all the earth!
You have set your glory above the heavens.

PSALM 8:1 NIV

Just as there comes a warm sunbeam into every cottage window, so comes a love—born of God's care for every separate need.

Nathaniel Hawthorne

My God shall supply all your need according
to His riches in glory by Christ Jesus.

PHILIPPIANS 4:19 NKJV

The King of Kings will raise His pierced hand and proclaim, "No more." The angels will stand and the Father will speak, "No more." Every person who lives and who ever lived will turn toward the sky and hear God announce, "No more." No more loneliness. No more tears. No more death. No more sadness. No more crying. No more pain.

Max Lucado

Then the angel...raised his right hand to heaven, and he made a
promise by the power of the One who lives forever and ever....
The angel promised, "There will be no more waiting!"

REVELATION 10:5-6 NCV

Let my soul take refuge...beneath the shadow of Your wings: let my heart, this sea of restless waves, find peace in You, O God.

Augustine

Let all who take refuge in you rejoice; let them sing
joyful praises forever. Spread your protection over them,
that all who love your name may be filled with joy.

PSALM 5:11 NLT

If instead of a gem, or even a flower, we should cast the gift of a loving thought into the heart of a friend, that would be giving as the angels give.

George MacDonald

My dear friend, it is good that you help the brothers and sisters,
even those you do not know.

3 John 1:5 ncv

As we practice the presence of God, more and more we find ourselves going through the stresses and strains of daily activity with an ease and serenity that amaze even us...especially us.

Richard J. Foster

*D*on't fret or worry. Instead of worrying, pray. Let petitions and praises shape your worries into prayers, letting God know your concerns. Before you know it, a sense of God's wholeness...will come and settle you down.

PHILIPPIANS 4:6-7 THE MESSAGE

*Millions of [angels] walk the earth unseen,
both when we sleep and when we wake.*

John Milton

Then he dreamed, and behold, a ladder was set up on the earth, and its top reached to heaven; and there the angels of God were ascending and descending on it.

GENESIS 28:12 NKJV

There is singing up in heaven such as we have never known,
Where the angels sing the praises of the Lamb upon the throne;
Their sweet harps are always tuneful and their voices always clear.
O, that we might be more like them while we serve the Master here.

Johnson Oatman Jr.

Rejoice with him, you heavens, and let all of God's angels worship him. Rejoice with his people, you nations, and let all the angels be strengthened in him.

DEUTERONOMY 32:43 NLT

Tuck [this] thought into your heart today. Treasure it. Your Father God cares about your daily everythings that concern you.

Kay Arthur

God will generously provide all you need. Then you will always have everything you need and plenty left over to share with others.

2 CORINTHIANS 9:8 NLT

Reputation is what men and women think of us. Character is what God and the angels know of us.

Thomas Paine

And what do you benefit if you gain the whole world but lose your own soul?
Is anything worth more than your soul? For the Son of Man will come with his angels
in the glory of his Father and will judge all people according to their deeds.

MATTHEW 16:26-27 NLT

All hail the power of Jesus' name! Let angels prostrate fall;
Bring forth the royal diadem, and crown Him Lord of all.

Edward Perronet

Without doubt, the secret of our life of worship is great: he was shown to us in a human body, proved right in spirit, and seen by angels. He was proclaimed to the nations, believed in by the world, and taken up in glory.

1 TIMOTHY 3:16 NCV

We encounter God in the ordinariness of life, not in the search for spiritual highs and extraordinary, mystical experiences, but in our simple presence in life.

Brennan Manning

*ake your everyday, ordinary life—your sleeping, eating, going-to-work,
and walking-around life—and place it before God as an offering.
Embracing what God does for you is the best thing you can do for him.*

ROMANS 12:1 THE MESSAGE

The guardian angels of life sometimes fly so high as to be beyond our sight, but they are always looking down upon us.

Jean Paul Richter

*The angel of the L*ORD *encamps around those who fear him, and he delivers them.*
*Taste and see that the L*ORD *is good; blessed is the man who takes refuge in him.*

PSALM 34:7-8 NIV

God is constantly taking knowledge of me in love,
and watching over me for my good.

J. I. Packer

*W*hat is man that You are mindful of him, and the son of man that
You visit him? For You have made him a little lower than the angels,
and You have crowned him with glory and honor.

PSALM 8:4-5 NKJV

*A*ngels and archangels may have gathered there,
Cherubim and seraphim thronged the air;
But His mother only, in her maiden bliss,
Worshipped the Beloved with a kiss.

Christina Rossetti

When God brings his firstborn into the world, he says,
"Let all God's angels worship him."

HEBREWS 1:6 NIV

God is the sunshine that warms us, the rain that melts the frost and waters the young plants. The presence of God is a climate of strong and bracing love, always there.

Joan Arnold

....

....

....

....

....

....

....

....

....

....

....

....

....

....

....

....

Let us acknowledge the LORD; let us press on to acknowledge him.
As surely as the sun rises, he will appear; he will come to us like the
winter rains, like the spring rains that water the earth.

HOSEA 6:3 NIV

We are His only witnesses. God is counting on each of us. No angel has been given the job. We are the lanterns—Christ is the light inside.

Oleta Spray

....

....

....

....

....

....

....

....

....

....

....

....

....

....

....

....

....

No one lights a lamp and then covers it with a bowl or hides it under a bed. A lamp is placed on a stand, where its light can be seen by all who enter the house.

LUKE 8:16 NLT

When home is ruled according to God's word, angels might be asked to stay with us, and they would not find themselves out of their element.

Charles H. Spurgeon

....

....

....

....

....

....

....

....

....

....

....

....

....

....

....

....

Keep on loving each other as brothers and sisters. Don't forget to show hospitality to strangers, for some who have done this have entertained angels without realizing it!

HEBREWS 13:1-2 NLT

Peace, perfect peace, with sorrows surging round?
In Jesus' presence naught but calm is found.
Peace, perfect peace, with loved ones far away?
In Jesus' keeping we are safe, and they.

E. H. Bickersteth

....

....

....

....

....

....

....

....

....

....

....

....

....

....

....

....

Go in peace. The presence of the Lord be with you on your way.

JUDGES 18:6 NKJV

*Look upon the skies, the earth, and the air as celestial joys...
as if you were among the angels.*

Thomas Traherne

At that time, the sign of the Son of Man will appear in the sky.... They will see the Son of Man coming on clouds in the sky with great power and glory. He will use a loud trumpet to send his angels all around the earth, and they will gather his chosen people from every part of the world.

MATTHEW 24:30-31 NCV

In the presence of hope—faith is born. In the presence of faith, love becomes a possibility! In the presence of love—miracles happen!

Robert Schuller

These three remain: faith, hope and love. But the greatest of these is love.

The empire of angels is as vast as God's creation.

Billy Graham

Hallelujah! Praise GOD from heaven, praise him from the mountaintops;
Praise him, all you his angels, praise him, all you his warriors,
Praise him, sun and moon, praise him, you morning stars.

PSALM 148:1-3 THE MESSAGE

Angels are God's representatives.... They protect us time after time in ways we are not even aware of.

Hope MacDonald

....

....

....

....

....

....

....

....

....

....

....

....

....

....

....

....

Don't you realize that I could ask my Father for thousands of angels to protect us, and he would send them instantly?

MATTHEW 26:53 NLT

The spiritual life is first of all a life. It is not merely something to be known and studied, it is to be lived.... We live as spiritual people when we live as people seeking God.

Thomas Merton

If you seek GOD, your God, you'll be able to find him if you're serious, looking for him with your whole heart and soul.

DEUTERONOMY 4:29 THE MESSAGE

A babe in the house is a wellspring of pleasure, a resting place for innocence on earth, a link between angels and man.

Sir Charles Tupper

From the lips of children and infants you have ordained praise.

PSALM 8:2 NIV

I feel from a spiritual standpoint that there's a real celebration of humanity, of the common bond of everybody. We need each other.

Amy Grant

*E*ncourage each other and build each other up,
just as you are already doing.

1 THESSALONIANS 5:11 NLT

God has made His children by adoption nearer
to Himself than the angels.

Thomas Watson

For I am persuaded that neither death nor life, nor angels nor principalities nor powers, nor things present nor things to come, nor height nor depth, nor any other created thing, shall be able to separate us from the love of God which is in Christ Jesus our Lord.

ROMANS 8:38-39 NKJV

It is not objective proof of God's existence that we want but the experience of God's presence. That is the miracle we are really after, and that is also, I think, the miracle that we really get.

Frederick Buechner

May you have the power to understand...how wide, how long, how high, and how deep his love is. May you experience the love of Christ, though it is too great to understand fully. Then you will be made complete with all the fullness of life and power that comes from God.

EPHESIANS 3:18-19 NLT

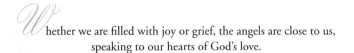

*W*hether we are filled with joy or grief, the angels are close to us,
speaking to our hearts of God's love.

Be joyful. Grow to maturity. Encourage each other. Live in harmony and peace.
Then the God of love and peace will be with you.

2 CORINTHIANS 13:11 NLT

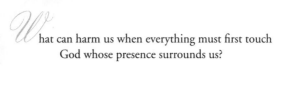
What can harm us when everything must first touch
God whose presence surrounds us?

If you make the LORD your refuge, if you make the Most High your shelter,
no evil will conquer you; no plague will come near your home.

PSALM 91:9-10 NLT

Angels are all around us, all the time, the divine power of their invisible wings moving through the very air we breathe.

....

....

....

....

....

....

....

....

....

....

....

....

....

....

....

....

Ever since the world was created, people have seen the earth and sky. Through everything God made, they can clearly see his invisible qualities—his eternal power and divine nature. So they have no excuse for not knowing God.

ROMANS 1:20 NLT

ove. No greater theme can be emphasized. No stronger message can be proclaimed. No finer song can be sung. No better truth can be imagined.

Charles R. Swindoll

$\mathcal{L}$ord, I will praise you among the nations; I will sing songs of praise about you to all the nations. Your great love reaches to the skies, your truth to the clouds.

PSALM 57:9-10 NCV

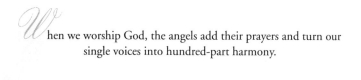

When we worship God, the angels add their prayers and turn our single voices into hundred-part harmony.

All heaven will praise your great wonders, LORD; myriads of angels
will praise you for your faithfulness.

PSALM 89:5 NLT

Angels are direct creations of God, each one a unique Master's piece.